All for Love

All for Love

SELECTED, EDITED AND ILLUSTRATED BY

Tasha Tudor

Philomel Books
New York

Copyright Acknowledgments

The editor and Philomel Books herewith render thanks to the following authors, publishers, and agents whose interest, cooperation, and permission to reprint have made possible the preparation of *All For Love*. All possible care has been taken to trace the ownership of every selection included and to make full acknowledgment for its use. If any errors have accidentally occurred, they will be corrected in subsequent editions, provided notification is sent to the publishers.

Farrar, Straus & Giroux, Inc., for an excerpt from *Break of Day*, by Colette. Copyright © 1961 by Martin Secker and Warburg Ltd. Reprinted by permission of Farrar, Straus & Giroux, Inc.

Houghton Mifflin Company for an excerpt from "Kokoro," by Lafcadio Hearne.

Hutchinson Publishing Group Ltd. for an extract from "The Corner of the Field," from *Collected Poems of Frances Cornford*. Reprinted by permission of Hutchinson Publishing Group Ltd.

J. M. Dent & Sons Ltd. for lines from the essay "A Love That Lasts," from *Searchlights and Nightingales*, by Robert Lynd. Reprinted by permission of J. M. Dent & Sons Ltd.

Macmillan Publishing Co., Ltd. for "Come," by Sara Teasdale, from *The Collected Poems of Sara Teasdale*. Reprinted by permission of Macmillan Publishing Co. Copyright © 1915 by Macmillan Publishing Co., Inc., renewed 1943 by Mamie T. Wheless.

Michael Yeats and Macmillan London Limited for the poem "The Song of Wandering Aengus," by W. B. Yeats. Reprinted by permission of A. P. Watt Ltd., agents, and Michael Yeats.

Norma Millay Ellis for the poem "Recuerdo," by Edna St. Vincent Millay, from *Collected Poems*, Harper & Row. Copyright © 1922, 1950 by Edna St. Vincent Millay. Reprinted by permission of Norma Millay Ellis.

Oxford University Press for the poem "Music I Heard," by Conrad Aiken, from *Collected Poems*. Copyright © 1953, 1970 by Conrad Aiken; renewed 1981 by Mary Aiken. Reprinted by permission of Oxford University Press, Inc.

Random House, Inc., and Alfred A. Knopf, Inc., for an extract from "Argonauta," from *Gift From the Sea*, by Anne Morrow Lindbergh. Copyright © 1955 by Anne Morrow Lindbergh. Reprinted by permission of Pantheon Books, a division of Random House, Inc.

Wesleyan University Press for "The Beautiful." Copyright © 1963 by W. H. Davies. Reprinted from *The Complete Poems of W. H. Davies* by permission of Wesleyan University Press.

Published by Philomel Books
a division of The Putnam Publishing Group
51 Madison Ave., New York, N.Y. 10010
Text copyright © 1984 by Philomel Books
Illustrations copyright © 1984 by Tasha Tudor
Printed in the United States of America
Designed by Nanette Stevenson/Calligraphy by Jeanyee Wong

Library of Congress Cataloging in Publication Data
Main entry under title: All for love.
Includes index.
Summary: An anthology of poems, stories, songs, letters, and
miscellaneous facts describing various aspects of love.
1. Love—Literary collections. [1. Love—Literary
collections] I. Tudor, Tasha.
PN6071.L7A4   1984   808.8'354   83-21959
ISBN 0-399-21012-1

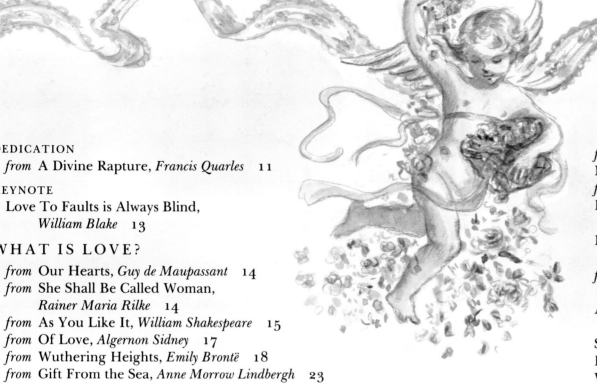

Contents

F.B.S.

For my Belovèd

If all those glittering monarchs that command
   The servile quarters of this earthly ball,
Should tender in exchange their shares of land,
   I would not change my fortunes for them all:
Their wealth is but a counter to my coin:
The world's but theirs; but my Belovèd's mine.

                      —*Francis Quarles*

Love to faults is always blind,
Always is to joy inclin'd
Lawless, wing'd, and unconfin'd.
And breaks all chains from every
    mind.

—*William Blake*

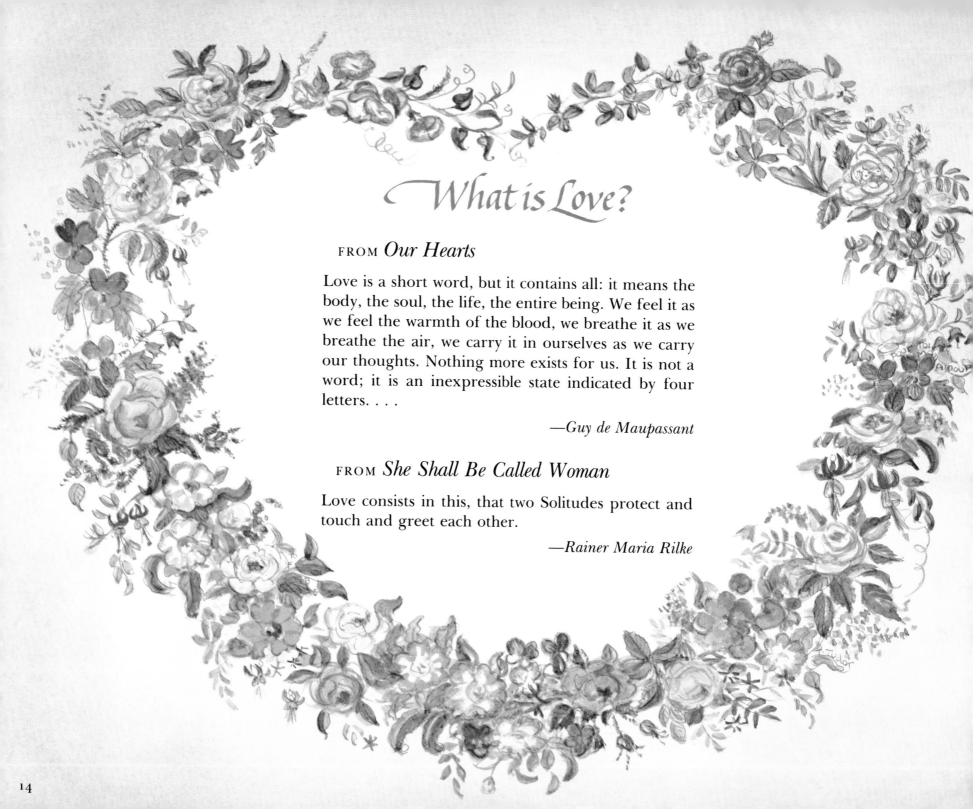

What is Love?

FROM *Our Hearts*

Love is a short word, but it contains all: it means the body, the soul, the life, the entire being. We feel it as we feel the warmth of the blood, we breathe it as we breathe the air, we carry it in ourselves as we carry our thoughts. Nothing more exists for us. It is not a word; it is an inexpressible state indicated by four letters. . . .

—*Guy de Maupassant*

FROM *She Shall Be Called Woman*

Love consists in this, that two Solitudes protect and touch and greet each other.

—*Rainer Maria Rilke*

FROM *As You Like It*

Phebe. Good shepherd, tell this youth what 'tis
     to love.
  Silvius. It is to be all made of sighs and tears . . .
It is to be all made of faith and service . . .
It is to be all made of fantasy,
All made of passion and all made of wishes,
All adoration, duty, and observance,
All humbleness, all patience and impatience,
All purity, all trial, all observance;
And so am I for Phebe.

                 —*William Shakespeare*

FROM *On Love*

Every promise of the soul has innumerable fulfil-
ments; each of its joys ripens into a new want. Nature,
uncontainable, flowing, forelooking, in the first senti-
ment of kindness anticipates already a benevolence
which shall lose all particular regards in its general
light. The introduction to this felicity is in a private
and tender relation of one to one, which is the en-
chantment of human life; which, like a certain divine
rage and enthusiasm, seizes on man at one period and
works a revolution in his mind and body; unites him
to his race, pledges him to the domestic and civic
relations, carries him with new sympathy into nature,
enhances the power of the senses, opens the imagination, adds to his character heroic and sacred at-
tributes, establishes marriage and gives permanence
to human society. . . . For it is a fire that kindling its
first embers in the narrow nook of a private bosom,
caught from a wandering spark out of another private heart, glows and enlarges until it warms and
beams upon multitudes of men and women, upon the
universal heart of all, and so lights up the whole
world and all nature with its generous flames.

—*Ralph Waldo Emerson*

FROM *Of Love*

Love is the most intensive desire of the soul to enjoy beauty, and, where it is reciprocal, is the most entire and exact union of hearts. . . . [Love] gives courage to the most fearful; sharpens the wit of the most simple; gives fidelity to the most depraved minds, constancy to the most unsettled; and, of itself alone, hath power to draw those hearts which have received it to acts of goodness, honesty, virtue, and gallantry, with more efficacy than all the most exact examples of history and philosophy. . . . The desire of a lover is to be loved, and that perfect union of hearts is the perfection of lovers' happiness. . . . as love is the cause of the greatest ills that men suffer, it is the cause also of the most perfect pleasures, consisting only in extremes; and as many as are made miserable by love, none are made happy without love.

—*Algernon Sidney*

FROM *Wuthering Heights*

I was rocking Hareton on my knee, and humming a song that began—

It was far in the night, and the bairnies grat,
The mither beneath the mools heard that,

when Miss Cathy, who had listened to the hubbub from her room, put her head in, and whispered—

"Are you alone, Nelly?"

"Yes, miss," I replied.

She entered and approached the hearth. I, supposing she was going to say something, looked up. The expression on her face seemed disturbed and anxious. Her lips were half asunder, as if she meant to speak, and she drew a breath; but it escaped in a sigh instead of a sentence.

I resumed my song; not having forgotten her recent behaviour. . . .

"Nelly, will you keep a secret for me?" she pursued, kneeling down by me, and lifting her winsome eyes to my face with that sort of look which turns off bad temper, even when one has all the right in the world to indulge it.

"Is it worth keeping?" I inquired, less sulkily.

"Yes, and it worries me, and I must let it out! I want to know what I should do. Today, Edgar Linton has asked me to marry him, and I've given him an answer. Now, before I tell you whether it was a consent or denial, you tell me what it ought to have been."

"Really, Miss Catherine, how can I know?" I replied. "To be sure, considering the exhibition you performed in his presence this afternoon, I might say it would be wise to refuse him: since he asked you after that, he must either be hopelessly stupid or a venturesome fool."

"If you talk so, I won't tell you any more," she returned, peevishly rising to her feet. "I accepted him, Nelly. Be quick, and say whether I was wrong!"

"You accepted him? Then what good is it discussing the matter? You have pledged your word, and cannot retract."

"But say whether I should have done so—do!" she exclaimed in an irritated tone; chafing her hands together, and frowning.

"There are many things to be considered before that question can be answered properly," I said, sententiously. "First and foremost, do you love Mr. Edgar?"

"Who can help it? Of course I do," she answered.

Then I put her through the following catechism: for a girl of twenty-two it was not injudicious.

"Why do you love him, Miss Cathy?"

"Nonsense, I do—that's sufficient."

"By no means; you must say why."

"Well, because he is handsome, and pleasant to be with."

"Bad!" was my commentary.

"And because he is young and cheerful."

"Bad, still."

"And because he loves me."

"Indifferent, coming there."

18

"And he will be rich, and I shall like to be the greatest woman of the neighbourhood, and I shall be proud of having such a husband."

"Worst of all! And now, say how you love him."

"As everybody loves—You're silly, Nelly."

"Not at all—Answer."

"I love the ground under his feet, and the air over his head, and everything he touches, and every word he says. I love all his looks, and all his actions, and him entirely and altogether. There now!"

"And why?"

"Nay, you are making a jest of it; it is exceedingly ill-natured! It's no jest to me!" said the young lady, scowling, and turning her face to the fire.

"I'm very far from jesting, Miss Catherine," I replied. "You love Mr. Edgar because he is handsome, and young, and cheerful, and rich, and loves you. The last, however, goes for nothing: you would love him without that, probably, and with it you wouldn't, unless he possessed the four former attractions."

"No, to be sure not; I should only pity him—hate him, perhaps, if he were ugly, and a clown."

"But there are several other handsome, rich young men in the world—handsomer, possibly, and richer than he is. What should hinder you from loving them?"

"If there be any, they are out of my way! I've seen none like Edgar."

"You may see some; and he won't always be handsome, and young, and may not always be rich."

"He is now; and I have only to do with the present. I wish you would speak rationally."

"Well, that settles it; if you have only to do with the present, marry Mr. Linton."

"I don't want your permission for that—I *shall* marry him; and yet you have not told me whether I'm right."

"Perfectly right; if people be right to marry only for the present. And now, let us hear what you are unhappy about. Your brother will be pleased; the old lady and gentleman will not object, I think; you will escape from a disorderly, comfortless home into a wealthy, respectable one; and you love Edgar, and Edgar loves you. All seems smooth and easy—where is the obstacle?"

"*Here!* and *here!*" replied Catherine, striking one hand on her forehead, and the other on her breast: "in whichever place the soul lives—in my soul, and in my heart, I'm convinced I'm wrong!" . . .

She seated herself by me again: her countenance grew sadder and graver, and her clasped hands trembled.

"Nelly, do you never dream queer dreams?" she said suddenly, after some minutes' reflection.

"Yes, now and then," I answered.

"And so do I. I've dreamt in my life dreams that have stayed with me ever after, and changed my ideas; they've gone through and through me, like wine through water, and altered the colour of my mind. And this is one—I'm going to tell it—but take care not to smile at any part of it."

"Oh don't, Miss Catherine!" I cried. "We're dismal enough without conjuring up ghosts, and visions to perplex us. Come, come, be merry, and like yourself! Look at little Hareton—*he's* dreaming nothing dreary. How sweetly he smiles in his sleep!"

"Yes; and how sweetly his father curses in his solitude! You remember him, I daresay, when he was just such another as that chubby thing—nearly as young and innocent. However, Nelly, I shall oblige you to listen—it's not long; and I've no power to be merry to-night."

"I won't hear it, I won't hear it!" I repeated, hastily.

I was superstitious about dreams then, and am still; and Catherine had an unusual gloom in her aspect, that made me dread something from which I might shape a prophecy, and foresee a fearful catastrophe.

She was vexed, but she did not proceed. Apparently taking up another subject, she recommenced in a short time:—

"If I were in heaven, Nelly, I should be extremely miserable."

"Because you are not fit to go there," I answered. "All sinners would be miserable in heaven."

"But it is not for that. I dreamt once that I was there."

"I tell you I won't hearken to your dreams, Miss Catherine! I'll go to bed," I interrupted again.

She laughed, and held me down, for I made a motion to leave my chair.

"This is nothing," cried she: "I was only going to say that heaven did not seem to be my home; and I broke my heart with weeping to come back to earth; and the angels were so angry that they flung me out into the middle of the heath on top of Wuthering Heights; where I woke sobbing for joy. That will do to explain my secret, as well as the other. I've no more business to marry Edgar Linton than I have to be in heaven; and if the wicked man in there had not brought Heathcliff so low, I shouldn't have thought of it. It would degrade me to marry Heathcliff, now; so he shall never know how I love him: and that, not because he's handsome, Nelly, but because he's more myself than I am. Whatever our souls are made of, his and mine are the same, and Linton's is as different as a moonbeam from lightning, or frost from fire.

". . . My love for Linton is like the foliage in the woods: time will change it, I'm well aware, as winter changes the trees—my love for Heathcliff resembles the eternal rocks beneath—a source of little visible delight, but necessary. Nelly, I *am* Heathcliff—he's always, always in my mind—not as a pleasure, any more than I am always a pleasure to myself—but, as my own being. . . ."

—*Emily Brontë*

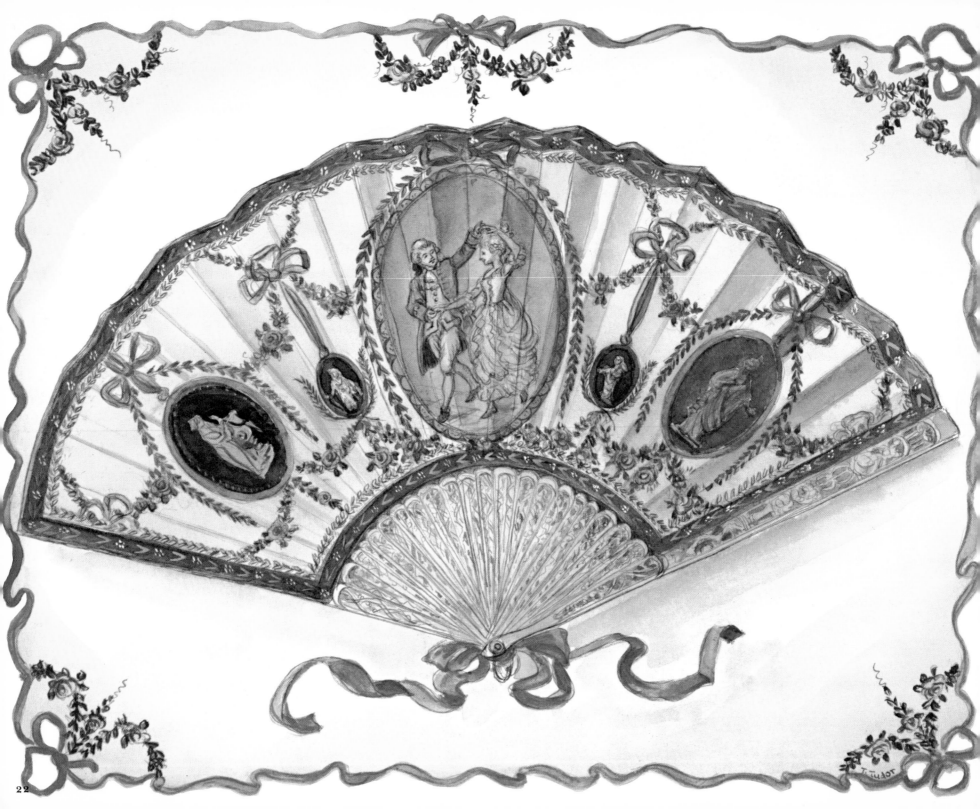

FROM *Gift From the Sea*

A good relationship has a pattern like a dance and is built on some of the same rules. The partners do not need to hold on tightly, because they move confidently in the same pattern, intricate but gay and swift and free, like a country dance of Mozart's. To touch heavily would be to arrest the pattern and freeze the movement, to check the endlessly changing beauty of its unfolding. There is no place here for the possessive clutch, the clinging arm, the heavy hand; only the barest touch in passing. Now arm in arm, now face to face, now back to back—it does not matter which. Because they know they are partners moving to the same rhythm, creating a pattern together, and being invisibly nourished by it.

The joy of such a pattern is not only the joy of creation or the joy of participation, it is also the joy of living in the moment. Lightness of touch and living in the moment are intertwined. One cannot dance well unless one is completely in time with the music, not leaning back to the last step or pressing forward to the next one, but poised directly on the present step as it comes. Perfect poise on the beat is what gives good dancing its sense of ease, of timelessness, of the eternal. It is what Blake was speaking of when he wrote:

He who bends to himself a joy
Doth the wingèd life destroy;
But he who kisses the joy as it flies
Lives in Eternity's sunrise.

The dancers who are perfectly in time never destroy "the wingèd life" in each other or in themselves. . . . When the heart is flooded with love there is no room in it for fear, for doubt, for hesitation. And it is this lack of fear that makes for the dance. When each partner loves so completely that he has forgotten to ask himself whether or not he is loved in return; when he only knows that he loves and is moving to its music—then, and then only, are two people able to dance perfectly in tune to the same rhythm.

—*Anne Morrow Lindbergh*

In Love

FROM *A Shepherd's Garland*

Love is my life, life is my love,
  love is my whole felicity,
Love is my sweet, sweet is my love,
  I am in love, and love in me.

—*Michael Drayton*

To My Dear and Loving Husband

If ever two were one, then surely we.
If ever man were loved by wife, then thee;
If ever wife was happy in a man,
Compare with me ye women if you can.
I prize thy love more than whole mines of gold,
Or all the riches that the East doth hold.
My love is such that rivers cannot quench,
Nor ought but love from thee give recompense.
Thy love is such I can no way repay;
The heavens reward thee manifold, I pray.
Then while we live, in love let's so persever,
That when we live no more we may love ever.

—*Anne Bradstreet (1678)*

Pack, Clouds, Away

Pack, clouds, away, and welcome day,
  With night we banish sorrow;
Sweet air blow soft, mount larks aloft
  To give my Love good-morrow!
Wings from the wind to please her mind
  Notes from the lark I'll borrow;
Bird, prune thy wing, nightingale sing,
  To give my Love good-morrow;
    To give my Love good-morrow
    Notes from them both I'll borrow.

Wake from thy nest, Robin-red-breast,
  Sing birds in every furrow;
And from each hill, let music shrill
  Give my fair Love good-morrow!
Blackbird and thrush in every bush,
  Stare, linnet, and cock-sparrow!
You pretty elves, amongst yourselves
  Sing my fair Love good-morrow;
    To give my Love good-morrow;
    Sing, birds, in every furrow.

                    —*Thomas Heywood*

A Birthday

My heart is like a singing bird
  Whose nest is in a watered shoot;
My heart is like an apple tree
  Whose boughs are bent
  with thickest fruit;
My heart is like a rainbow shell
  That paddles in a halcyon sea;
My heart is gladder than all these
  Because my love is come to me.

Raise me a dais of silk and down;
  Hang it with vair and purple dyes;
Carve it in doves, and pomegranates,
  And peacocks with a hundred eyes;
Work it in gold and silver grapes,
  In leaves, and silver fleurs-de-lys;
Because the birthday of my life
  Is come, my love is come to me.
                    —*Christina Rossetti*

How Do I Love Thee?

How do I love thee? Let me count the ways.
I love thee to the depth and breadth and height
My soul can reach, when feeling out of sight
For the ends of Being and ideal Grace.
I love thee to the level of everyday's
Most quiet need, by sun and candle-light.
I love thee freely, as men strive for Right;
I love thee purely, as they turn from Praise.
I love thee with the passion put to use
In my old griefs, and with my childhood's faith.
I love thee with a love I seemed to lose
With my lost saints,—I love thee with the breath,
Smiles, tears, of all my life!—and, if God choose,
I shall but love thee better after death.

—*Elizabeth Barrett Browning*

27

To the growing youth, whose life is normal and vigorous, there comes a sort of atavistic period in which he begins to feel for the feebler sex that primitive contempt created by mere consciousness of physical superiority. But it is just at the time when the society of girls has grown least interesting to him that he suddenly becomes insane. There crosses his life-path a maiden never seen before,—but little different from other daughters of men,—not at all wonderful to common vision. At the same instant, with a single surging shock, the blood rushes to his heart; and all his senses are bewitched. Thereafter, till the madness ends, his life belongs wholly to that new-found being, of whom he yet knows nothing, except that the sun's light seems more beautiful when it touches her. From that glamour no mortal science can disenthrall him.

—*Lafcadio Hearn*

Recuerdo

We were very tired, we were very merry—
We had gone back and forth all night on the ferry.
It was bare and bright, and smelled like a stable—
But we looked into a fire, we leaned across a table,
We lay on a hill-top underneath the moon;
And the whistles kept blowing, and the dawn came soon.

We were very tired, we were very merry—
We had gone back and forth all night on the ferry;
And you ate an apple, and I ate a pear,
From a dozen of each we had bought somewhere;
And the sky went wan, and the wind came cold,
And the sun rose dripping, a bucketful of gold.

We were very tired, we were very merry,
We had gone back and forth all night on the ferry.
We hailed, "Good morrow, mother!"
  to a shawl-covered head,
And bought a morning paper, which neither of us read;
And she wept, "God bless you!" for the apples and pears,
And we gave her all our money but our subway fares.

—*Edna St. Vincent Millay*

Your Hands Lie Open

Your hands lie open in the long fresh grass,—
The finger-points look through like rosy blooms:
Your eyes smile peace. The pasture gleams
   and glooms
'Neath billowing skies that scatter and amass.
All round our nest, far as the eye can pass,
Are golden kingcup-fields with silver edge
Where the cow-parsley skirts the hawthorn-hedge.
'Tis visible silence, still as the hour-glass.
Deep in the sun-searched growths the dragon-fly
Hangs like a blue thread loosened from the sky:—
So this winged hour is dropped to us from above.
Oh! clasp we to our hearts, for deathless dower,
This close-companioned inarticulate hour
When twofold silence was the song of love.

—*Dante Gabriel Rossetti*

The Corner of the Field

Here the young lover, on his elbow raised,
Looked at his happy girl with grass surrounded,
And flicked the spotted beetle from her wrist:
She, with head thrown back, at heaven gazed,
At Suffolk clouds, serene and slow and mounded;
Then calmly smiled at him before they kissed.

—*Frances Cornford*

Come

Come, when the pale moon like a petal
   Floats in the pearly dusk of Spring,
Come with arms outstretched to take me,
   Come with lips that long to cling.

Come, for life is a frail moth flying,
   Caught in the web of the years that pass.
And soon we two, so warm and eager,
   Will be as the gray stones in the grass.

                  —*Sara Teasdale*

Love Song

The honey of the Hybla bees
Is not so sweet as kissing you;
Nor autumn wind in dying trees
So wistful is as missing you.

And when you are not mine to kiss,
My every thought is haunting you,
And when your mouth is mine, I miss
The wistfulness of wanting you.

                  —*Samuel Hoffenstein*

For "G"

All night under the moon
Plovers are flying
Over the dreaming meadows of silvery light,
Over the meadows of June
Flying and crying—
Wandering voices of love in the hush of the night.

All night under the moon
Love, though we're lying
Quietly under the thatch, in the silvery light
Over the meadows of June
Together we're flying—
Rapturous voices of love in the hush of the night.

                  —*Wilfrid Gibson*

FROM *Hamlet*

Doubt thou the stars are fire;
   Doubt that the sun doth move,
Doubt truth to be a liar;
   But never doubt I love.

                  —*William Shakespeare*

Shall I Compare thee to a Summers Day?

Shall I compare thee to a Summers day?
Thou art more lovely and more temperate:
Rough windes do shake the darling buds of Maie,
And Sommers lease hath all too short a date:
Sometime too hot the eye of heaven shines,
And often is his gold complexion dimm'd,
And every faire from faire some-time declines,
By chance, or natures changing course untrim'd:
But thy eternall Sommer shall not fade,
Nor lose possession of that faire thou ow'st,
Nor shall death brag thou wandr'st in his shade,
When in eternall lines to time thou grow'st,
    So long as men can breath or eyes can see,
    So long lives this, and this gives life to thee.

—William Shakespeare

Meeting at Night

The gray sea and the long black land;
And the yellow half-moon large and low;
And the startled little waves that leap
In fiery ringlets from their sleep,
As I gain the cove with pushing prow,
And quench its speed i' the slushy sand.

Then a mile of warm sea-scented beach;
Three fields to cross till a farm appears;
A tap at the pane, the quick sharp scratch
And blue spurt of a lighted match,
And a voice less loud, thro' its joys and fears,
Than the two hearts beating each to each!

—Robert Browning

FROM *Dover Beach*

Ah, love, let us be true
To one another! for the world, which seems
To lie before us like a land of dreams,
So various, so beautiful, so new,
Hath really neither joy, nor love, nor light,
Nor certitude, nor peace, nor help for pain;
And we are here as on a darkling plain
Swept with confused alarms of struggle and flight,
Where ignorant armies clash by night.

—*Matthew Arnold*

A Girl with Jade Eyes

A girl with jade eyes
Leans on the wall of a pavilion.
She has the moonrise in her heart
And the singing of love songs
Comes to her up the river.

She stands and dreams for me
Outside the house by the bamboo door.
In a minute
I will leave my shadow
And talk to her of poetry and love.

—*Song of Annam (Anonymous)*

Do Not Smile to Yourself

Do not smile to yourself
Like a green mountain
With a cloud drifting across it.
People will know we are in love.

—*Lady Otomo of Sakanoe*

If Thou Must Love Me

If thou must love me, let it be for naught
Except for love's sake only. Do not say,
'I love her for her smile—her look—her way
Of speaking gently,—for a trick of thought
That falls in well with mine, and certes brought
A sense of pleasant ease on such a day'—
For these things in themselves, Belovèd, may
Be changed, or change for thee—and love,
    so wrought,
May be unwrought so. Neither love me for
Thine own dear pity's wiping my cheeks dry:
A creature might forget to weep, who bore
Thy comfort long, and lose thy love thereby!
But love me for love's sake, that evermore
Thou mayst love on, through love's eternity.

—*Elizabeth Barrett Browning*

White

I thought that it was snowing
Flowers. But, no. It was this young lady
Coming towards me.

—*Yori-Kito*

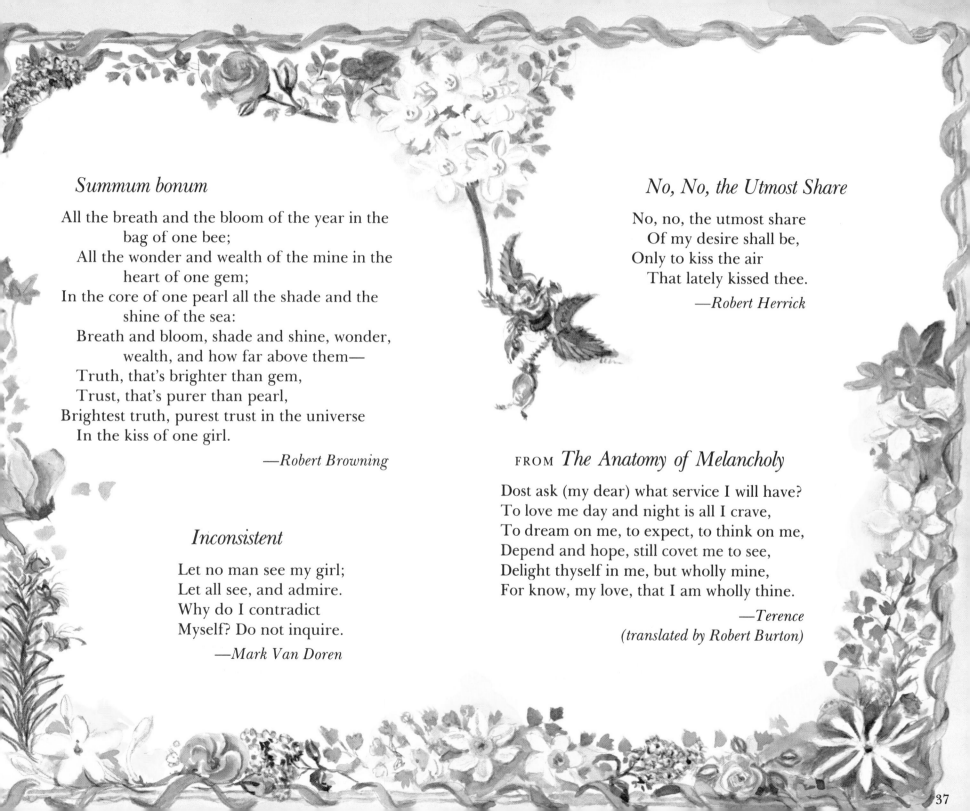

Summum bonum

All the breath and the bloom of the year in the
    bag of one bee;
    All the wonder and wealth of the mine in the
    heart of one gem;
In the core of one pearl all the shade and the
    shine of the sea:
    Breath and bloom, shade and shine, wonder,
    wealth, and how far above them—
Truth, that's brighter than gem,
Trust, that's purer than pearl,
Brightest truth, purest trust in the universe
    In the kiss of one girl.

                —*Robert Browning*

Inconsistent

Let no man see my girl;
Let all see, and admire.
Why do I contradict
Myself? Do not inquire.

         —*Mark Van Doren*

No, No, the Utmost Share

No, no, the utmost share
    Of my desire shall be,
Only to kiss the air
    That lately kissed thee.

        —*Robert Herrick*

FROM *The Anatomy of Melancholy*

Dost ask (my dear) what service I will have?
To love me day and night is all I crave,
To dream on me, to expect, to think on me,
Depend and hope, still covet me to see,
Delight thyself in me, but wholly mine,
For know, my love, that I am wholly thine.

            —*Terence*
(translated by Robert Burton)

You'll Love Me Yet

You'll love me yet!—and I can tarry
　　Your love's protracted growing:
June rear'd that bunch of flowers you carry,
　　From seeds of April's sowing.

I plant a heartful now; some seed
　　At least is sure to strike,
And yield—what you'll not pluck indeed,
　　Not love, but, maybe, like.

You'll look at least on love's remains,
　　A grave's one violet:
Your look?—that pays a thousand pains.
　　What's death? You'll love me yet!

　　　　　　　　　　　—*Robert Browning*

Enduring Love

FROM *When You Are Old*

When you are old and grey and full of sleep,
And nodding by the fire, take down this book,
And slowly read, and dream of the soft look
Your eyes had once, and of their shadows deep;
How many loved your moments of glad grace,
And loved your beauty, with love false or true,
But one man loved the pilgrim soul in you,
And loved the sorrows of your changing face.

—*William Butler Yeats*

FROM *His Mother's Wedding Ring*

The ring, so worn as you behold,
So thin, so pale, is yet of gold:
The passion such it was to prove—
Worn with life's care, love yet was love.

—*George Crabbe*

Oh, No—
Not Ev'n When First We Lov'd

Oh, no—not ev'n when first we lov'd
    Wert thou as dear as now thou art;
Thy beauty then my senses mov'd.
    But now thy virtues bind my heart.
What was but Passion's sign before
    Has since been turn'd to Reason's vow;
And, though I then might love thee *more*,
    Trust me, I love thee *better* now.

Although my heart in earlier youth
    Might kindle with more wild desire,
Believe me, it has gain'd in truth
    Much more than it has lost in fire.
The flame now warms my inmost core
    That then but sparkled o'er my brow,
And though I seem'd to love thee more,
    Yet, oh, I love thee better now.

—*Thomas Moore*

Secret Love

Renouncement

I must not think of thee; and, tired yet strong,
I shun the thought that lurks in all delight—
The thought of thee—and in the blue heaven's height,
And in the dearest passage of a song.
Oh, just beyond the fairest thoughts that throng
This breast, the thought of thee waits, hidden yet bright
But it must never, never come in sight;
I must stop short of thee the whole day long.
But when sleep comes to close each difficult day,
When night gives pause to the long watch I keep,
And all my bonds I needs must loose apart,
Must doff my will as raiment laid away,—
With the first dream that comes with the first sleep
I run, I run, I am gathered to thy heart.

—*Alice Meynell*

I Hid My Love

I hid my love when young till I
Couldn't hear the buzzing of a fly;
I hid my love to my despite
Till I could not bear to look at light:
I dare not gaze upon her face
But left her memory in each place;
Where'er I saw a wild flower lie
I kissed and bade my love good-bye.

I met her in the greenest dells,
Where dewdrops pearl the wood bluebells;
The lost breeze kissed her bright blue eye,
The bee kissed and went singing by,
A sunbeam found a passage there,
A gold chain round her neck so fair;
As secret as the wild bee's song
She lay there all the summer long.

I hid my love in field and town
Till e'en the breeze would knock me down,
The bees seemed singing ballads o'er,
The fly's bass turned a lion's roar;
And even silence found a tongue,
To haunt me all the summer long;
The riddle nature could not prove
Was nothing else but secret love.

—*John Clare*

FROM *The Little Minister*

Long ago when our caged blackbirds never saw a king's soldier without whistling impudently, "Come over the water to Charlie" a minister of Thrums was to be married, but something happened, and he remained a bachelor. Then when he was old, he passed in our square the lady who was to have been his wife, and her hair was white, but she, too, was still unmarried. The meeting had only one witness, a weaver, and he said solemnly afterwards, "They did not speak, but they just gave one another a look, and I saw the love light in their eyes." No more is remembered of these two, no being now living ever saw them, but the poetry that was in the soul of a battered weaver makes them human to us forever.

—*J. M. Barrie*

The Song of the Wandering Aengus

I went out to the hazel wood,
Because a fire was in my head,
And cut and peeled a hazel wand,
And hooked a berry to a thread;
And when white moths were on the wing,
And moth-like stars were flickering out,
I dropped the berry in a stream
And caught a little silver trout.

When I had laid it on the floor
I went to blow the fire aflame,
But something rustled on the floor,
And some one called me by my name:
It had become a glimmering girl
With apple blossom in her hair
Who called me by my name and ran
And faded through the brightening air.

Though I am old with wandering
Through hollow lands and hilly lands,
I will find out where she has gone,
And kiss her lips and take her hands;
And walk among long dappled grass,
And pluck till time and times are done
The silver apples of the moon,
The golden apples of the sun.

—*William Butler Yeats*

Other Loves

The Love of Friends

Happy is the house that shelters a friend! It might well be built, like a festal bower or arch, to entertain him a single day.... I awoke this morning with devout thanksgiving for my friends, the old and the new.... High thanks I owe you, excellent lovers, who carry out the world for me to new and noble depths, and enlarge the meaning of all my thoughts....

There are two elements that go to the composition of friendship, each so sovereign that I can detect no superiority in either, no reason why either should be first named. One is truth. A friend is a person with whom I may be sincere. Before him I may think aloud. I . . . may deal with him with the simplicity and wholeness with which one chemical atom meets another....

The other element of friendship is tenderness.... Can another be so blessed and we so pure that we can offer him tenderness? When a man becomes dear to me I have touched the goal of fortune.... I feel as warmly when he is praised, as the lover when he hears applause of his engaged maiden.... His goodness seems better than our goodness, his nature finer, his temptations less. Every thing that is his—his name, his form, his dress, books and instruments—fancy enhances. Our own thought sounds new and larger from his mouth....

In the last analysis, love is only the reflection of a man's own worthiness from other men.... The only reward of virtue is virtue; the only way to have a friend is to be one....

—*Ralph Waldo Emerson*

The Love of Money

Those who save money are often accused of loving money; but, in my opinion, those who love money most are those who spend it. To them money is not merely a list of dead figures in a bankbook. It is an animate thing, spasmodically restless like the birds in a wood, taking wings to itself, as the poet has said. Money, to the man who enjoys spending, is the perfect companion—a companion all the dearer because it never outstays its welcome.

—*Robert Rynd*

FROM
The Rime of the Ancient Mariner

He prayeth best, who loveth best
All things both great and small;
For the dear God who loveth us,
He made and loveth all.

—*Samuel Taylor Coleridge*

Upon His Spaniel Tracy

Now thou art dead, no eye shall ever see,
For shape and service, spaniel like to thee.
This shall my love do, give thy sad death one
Tear, that deserves of me a million.

—*Robert Herrick*

Love of Family

FROM *My Mother's House*

Sir,

You ask me to come and spend a week with you, which means I would be near my daughter, whom I adore. You who live with her know how rarely I see her, how much her presence delights me, and I'm touched that you should ask me to come and see her. All the same I'm not going to accept your kind invitation, for the time being at any rate. The reason is that my pink cactus is probably going to flower. It's a very rare plant I've been given, and I'm told that in our climate it flowers only once every four years. Now, I am already a very old woman, and if I went away when my pink cactus is about to flower, I am certain I shouldn't see it flower again.

So I beg you, Sir, to accept my sincere thanks and my regrets, together with my kind regards.

This note, signed *"Sidonie Colette, née Landoy,"* was written by my mother to one of my husbands, the second. A year later she died, at the age of seventy-seven.

Whenever I feel myself inferior to everything about me, threatened by my own mediocrity, frightened by the discovery that a muscle is losing its strength, a desire its power or a pain the keen edge of its bite, I can still hold up my head and say to myself: "I am the daughter of the woman who wrote that letter—that letter and so many more that I have kept. This one tells me in ten lines that at the age of seventy-six she was planning journeys and undertaking them, but that waiting for the possible bursting into bloom of a tropical flower held everything up and silenced even her heart, made for love. I am the daughter of a woman who, in a mean, close-fisted, confined little place, opened her village home to stray cats, tramps and pregnant servant-girls. I am the daughter of a woman who many a time, when she was in despair at not having enough money for others, ran through the wind-whipped snow to cry from door to door, at the houses of the rich, that a child had just been born in a poverty-stricken home to parents whose feeble, empty hands had no swaddling clothes for it. Let me not forget that I am the daughter of a woman who bent her head, trembling, between the blades of a cactus, her wrinkled face full of ecstacy over the promise of a flower, a woman who herself never ceased to flower, untiringly, during three quarters of a century."

—*Colette*

The Beautiful

Three things there are more beautiful
   Than any man could wish to see:
The first, it is a full-rigged ship
   Sailing with all her sails set free;
The second, when the wind and sun
   Are playing in a field of corn;
The third, a woman, young and fair,
   Showing her child before it is born.

                     —*W. H. Davies*

FROM *The Goblin Market*

For there is no friend like a sister
In calm or stormy weather;
To cheer one on the tedious way,
To fetch one if one goes astray,
To lift one if one totters down,
To strengthen whilst one stands.

—*Christina Rossetti*

Ah My Dear Son

"Ah, my dear, ah my dear son,"
    Said Mary, "ah my dear,
Kiss thy mother, Jesu,
    With a laughing cheer."

—*Anonymous*

Love in Absence

Music I Heard

Music I heard with you was more than music,
And bread I broke with you was more than bread;
Now that I am without you, all is desolate;
All that was once so beautiful is dead.

Your hands once touched this table and this silver,
And I have seen your fingers hold this glass.
These things do not remember you, belovèd,—
And yet your touch upon them will not pass.

For it was in my heart you moved among them,
And blessed them with your hands and with your eyes
And in my heart they will remember always,—
They knew you once, O beautiful and wise.

—Conrad Aiken

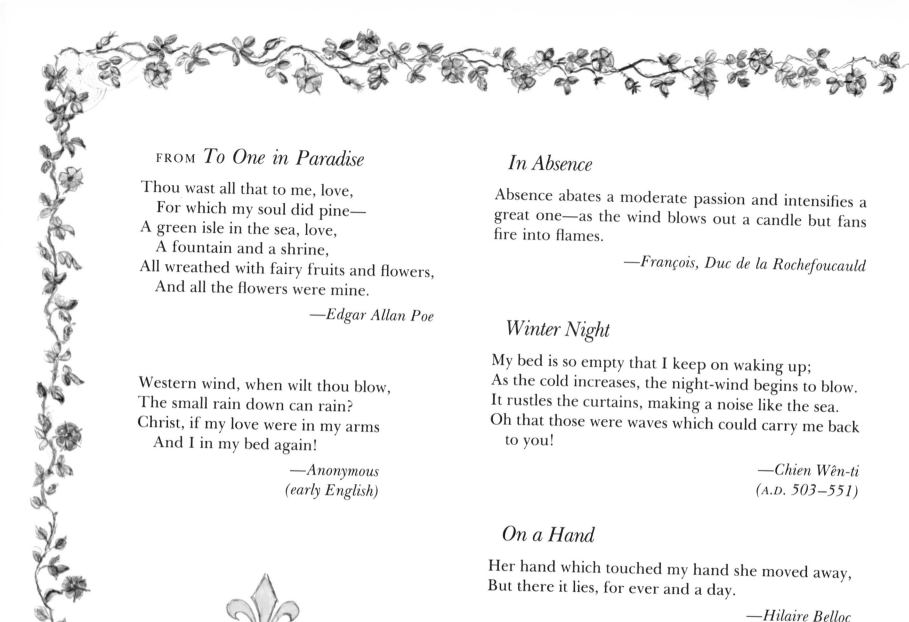

FROM *To One in Paradise*

Thou wast all that to me, love,
    For which my soul did pine—
A green isle in the sea, love,
    A fountain and a shrine,
All wreathed with fairy fruits and flowers,
    And all the flowers were mine.

—Edgar Allan Poe

Western wind, when wilt thou blow,
The small rain down can rain?
Christ, if my love were in my arms
    And I in my bed again!

—Anonymous
(early English)

In Absence

Absence abates a moderate passion and intensifies a
great one—as the wind blows out a candle but fans
fire into flames.

—François, Duc de la Rochefoucauld

Winter Night

My bed is so empty that I keep on waking up;
As the cold increases, the night-wind begins to blow.
It rustles the curtains, making a noise like the sea.
Oh that those were waves which could carry me back
    to you!

—Chien Wên-ti
(A.D. 503–551)

On a Hand

Her hand which touched my hand she moved away,
But there it lies, for ever and a day.

—Hilaire Belloc

Love Letters

General Napoleon Bonaparte to Citizeness Josephine Bonaparte

Not a word from you; good God! What have I done? To think only of you, to love only Josephine, to live for nothing but my wife, to enjoy nothing but the happiness of my beloved, does all that earn me such harsh treatment? My love, please, think of me often and write to me every day. You must be ill, or else you don't love me! Do you think my heart is made of marble?

My one and only Josephine, apart from you there is no joy; away from you the world is a desert where I am alone and cannot open my heart. You have taken more than my soul; you are the one thought of my life. When I am tired of the worry of work, when I fear the outcome, when men annoy me, when I am ready to curse being alive, I put my hand on my heart; your portrait hangs there, I look at it, and love brings me perfect happiness. . . . Oh, my adorable wife! I don't know what fate has in store for me, but if it keeps me apart from you any longer, it will be unbearable! My courage is not enough for that. Come and join me; before we die let us at least be able to say: "We had so many happy days!!"

Catherine of Aragon to Henry VIII

My most dear lord, king, and husband,

The hour of my death now approaching, I cannot choose but out of love I bear you to advise you of your soul's health, which you ought to prefer before all considerations of the world or flesh whatsoever. For which yet you have cast me into many calamities, and yourself into many troubles. But I forgive you all; and pray God to do so likewise. For the rest I commend unto you Mary, our daughter, beseeching you to be a good father unto her, as I have heretofore desired. I must intreat you also, to respect my maids, and give them in marriage, which is not much, they being but three; and to all my other servants a year's pay, besides their due, lest otherwise they should be unprovided for; lastly I make this vow, that mine eyes desire you above all things. Farewell.

Percy Bysshe Shelley to Mary Godwin Shelley

Bagni di Lucca,
Sunday Morning, 23rd August, 1818.

My dearest Mary,

We arrived here last night at twelve o'clock, and it is now before breakfast the next morning. I can of course tell you nothing of the future, and though I shall not close this letter till post-time, yet I do not know exactly when that is. Yet, if you are still very impatient, look along the letter, and you will see another date, when I may have something to relate. . . . Well, but the time presses. I am now going to the banker's to send you money for the journey, which I shall address to you at Florence, Post Office. Pray come instantly to Este, where I shall be waiting in the utmost anxiety for your arrival. . . .

Do you know, dearest, how this letter was written? By scrap and patches and interrupted every minute. The gondola is now coming to take me to the banker's. Este is a little place and the house found without difficulty. I shall count four days for this letter, one day for packing, four for coming here—and the ninth or tenth day we shall meet.

I am too late for the post, but I send an express to overtake it. Enclosed is an order for fifty pounds. If you knew all that I have to do! Dearest love, be well, be happy, come to me. Confide in your own constant and affectionate

P.B.S.

Kiss the blue-eyed darlings* for me, and do not let William forget me. Clara cannot recollect me.

*Their son and baby daughter.

George Gordon, Lord Byron to the Countess Guiccioli

Bologna, August 25, 1819.

My Dearest Teresa,—I have read this book in your garden;—my love, you were absent, or else I could not have read it. It is a favourite book of yours, and the writer was a friend of mine. You will not understand these English words, and *others* will not understand them,—which is the reason I have not scrawled them in Italian. But you will recognize the handwriting of him who passionately loved you, and you will divine that, over a book which was yours, he could only think of love.

In that word, beautiful in all languages, but most so in yours—*Amor mio*—is comprised my existence here and hereafter. I feel I exist here, and I feel that I shall exist hereafter,—to *what* purpose you will decide; my destiny rests with you, and you are a woman, eighteen years of age, and two out of a convent, I wish that you had staid there, with all my heart,—or, at least, that I had never met you in your married state.

But all this is too late. I love you, and you love me,—at least, you say so, and act as if you *did* so, which last is a great consolation in all events. But *I* more than love you, and cannot cease to love you.

Think of me, sometimes, when the Alps and ocean divide us,—but they never will, unless you wish it.

Byron

Michael Faraday to Sarah Barnard

Royal Institution: Thursday evening
[December, 1820]

My dear Sarah—It is astonishing how much the state of the body influences the powers of the mind. I have been thinking all morning of the very delightful and interesting letter I would send you this evening, and now I am so tired, and yet have so much to do, that my thoughts are quite giddy, and run round your image without any power of themselves to stop and admire it. I want to say a thousand kind and, believe me, heartfelt things to you, but am not master of words fit for the purpose;* and still, as I ponder and think on you, chlorides, oil, Davy, steel, miscellanea, mercury, and fifty other professional fancies swim before and drive me further and further into the quandary of stupidness.

*From your affectionate
Michael*

* Despite Michael Faraday's asserted inability to write a proper love letter, he and Sarah Barnard were later married!

Sarah Bernhardt to Victorien Sardou

Wonderful Boy,

Where are you to-night? Your letter came only an hour ago—cruel hour—I had hoped you would spend it with me here.

Paris is a morgue without you: before I knew you, it was Paris, and I thought it heaven; but now it is a vast desert of desolation and loneliness. It is like the face of a clock, bereft of its hands.

All the pictures that hung in my memory before I knew you have faded and given place to our radiant moments together.

Now I cannot live apart from you; your words, even though bitter, dispel all the cares of the world and make me happy; my art has been suckled by them and softly rocked in their tender cradle; they are as necessary to me now as sunlight and air.

I am hungry for them as for food, I am thirsty for them, and my thirst is overwhelming. *Your words are my food, your breath my wine. You are everything to me.*

Your Sarah.

John Keats to Fanny Brawne

My dearest Girl,

This moment I have set myself to copy some verses out fair. I cannot proceed with any degree of content. I must write you a line or two and see if that will assist in dismissing you from my mind for ever so short a time. Upon my soul I can think of nothing else. The time is passed when I had power to advise and warn you against the unpromising morning of my Life. My love has made me selfish. I cannot exist without you. I am forgetful of everything but seeing you again—my life seems to stop there—I see no further. You have absorbed me. I have a sensation at the present moment as though I was dissolving—I should be exquisitely miserable without the hope of soon seeing you. I should be afraid to separate myself far from you. My sweet Fanny, will your heart never change? My love, will it? I have no limit now to my love. . . .

I have been astonished that Men could die Martyrs for religion—I have shuddered at it. I shudder no more—I could be martyred for my religion—love is my religion—I could die for that. I could die for you. My Creed is Love and you are its only tenet. You have ravished me away by a Power I cannot resist; and yet I could resist till I saw you; and even since I have seen you I have endeavoured often to reason against the reasons of my love. I can do that no more—the pain would be too great. My love is selfish. I cannot breathe without you.

Yours for ever,
John Keats.

Love and Kisses

Love potions and charms, and other folkloric wisdoms about love

If two girls break the wishbone of a chicken or turkey between them, they can find out which one will be the first to marry. Each must hold one of the branches of the bone with the little finger of her right hand; then they must pull until the bone snaps. The one with the shorter piece will marry soonest. There is an old rhyme:

Shortest to marry,
Longest will tarry.

They say that a cake made of wheat flour, amaranth seeds and the first honey from a new hive will make your true love propose to you. In the old days, the recipe included the heart of a white dove, dried and powdered, but it has been found to work without this ingredient.

Rose leaves and forget-me-nots made into tea are also effective in making your loved one love you.

My grandmother told me that if you can peel an apple so that the peel is all in one long piece, and then throw the peel over your left shoulder onto the floor, it will form the initial of the person you will marry.

When you go to a wedding, take a little piece of the wedding cake home with you and put it under your pillow; you will dream about the person you will marry. Some people say that the same result will be obtained by putting a silver spoon or a mirror under your pillow, but the wedding cake is the surest bringer of the information you want.

Four-leaved clovers always bring good luck. But if you find four of them, and put one beneath each corner of your bedsheet, you will dream of the person you will marry. Good luck, indeed!

You can find out if the person you love loves you by pulling off the petals of a daisy or black-eyed Susan while you say:

He (or she) loves me,
He loves me not,
He loves me,
He loves me not,
He loves me, . . . etc.
The last petal will tell you the answer.

Kisses

from *Cyrano de Bergerac:*
And what is a kiss when all is done?
A rosy dot over the "i" of loving . . .

—*Edmund Rostand*

The ancient Romans asked the same question: *Sacchro quid superat? Libum. Quid libo? Favorum Gustus. At hunc gustum? Basia roscidula.*
(What is better than sugar?—Honey-cake. Than honey-cake?—The flavor of honey-combs. Than this flavor?—Dewy kisses—)

There are many quaint sayings about kisses. For example in Germany there is said to be nothing in a kiss without a beard: *Ein Kuss ohne Bart ist eine Vesper ohne Magnificat* (A kiss without a beard is like Vespers without the Magnificat); or, still more strongly, *Ein Kuss ohne Bart ist ein Ei ohne Salz* (A kiss without a beard is like an egg without salt). The young girls in Holland also incline to this point of view: *Een kussje zonder baard, een eitje zonder zout* (. . . an egg without salt), and they have in the Frisian Islands some who share their taste: *An Kleeb sanner Biard as äs en Brei sanner Salt* (. . . porridge without salt).

As the living expression of the warmest and sincerest human feelings, kissing has been credited, in the world of fairy tales and superstition, with a considerable curative and healing power.

In the old sagas and ballads, enchantments are broken by means of a kiss; holy men in legends restore the sick to health by means of a kiss. Kissing has also given rise to many superstitious notions of which here are a few:

To protect yourself against lightning, make three

crosses before you, and kiss the ground three times. (*Germany*)

To protect yourself in gambling, kiss the cards before the game begins. (*France*)

To cure a toothache, kiss a donkey on his chops. (*Germany*) This very efficacious advice is found as far back as Pliny.

If you drop a bit of bread on the floor you must kiss it when you pick it up. The same respect is also to be shown to books you have dropped. (*Denmark and Germany*)

People kiss little children when they have hurt themselves, in order to take away the pain; they must "kiss the place and make it well."

A kiss is expressive of love in the widest and most comprehensive meaning of the word. It can bring a message of loyal affection, gratitude, compassion, sympathy, intense joy, and profound sorrow.

A kiss is the expression of the deep and intense feeling that knits parents to their offspring. At its entrance into the world, the little helpless infant is received by its father's and mother's warm kiss. In the Middle Ages they kissed the newborn baby three times in the name of the Holy Trinity.

In Homer's *Iliad,* when Hector takes leave of his wife Andromache, he lifts his little son up into his arms, but the child is afraid of his father's helmet, "of the gleam of the copper and the nodding crest of horse-hair."

> And from his brow Hector removed the casque,
> and set it down, all glittering, on the ground;
> then kissed his child, and danced him in his arms.

The kiss at the end of the wedding ceremony is regarded as the introduction, as it were, to married life. This tradition is an ancient one and has even come to be part of the law in some countries. Italy is the Western European country where *donatio propter osculum* has been longest retained. We find, even down to our own times, traces of the same in customary laws.

This is probably the only ceremonial kiss that has received legal sanction; but wherever elsewhere we

may turn our eyes and investigate old ceremonies, we constantly find the kiss a necessary and important part.

For instance in medieval Britain, and even later, at the ceremony of dubbing a knight, the newly made knight of the Golden Fleece was kissed by the master of the ceremony, and had afterwards to kiss all the senior knights present.

At certain academic functions the kiss also formed part of the ceremony; in the seventeenth century, the Dean, when degrees were conferred, kissed all the new doctors and masters.

It is easily understood that the kiss likewise came to play a prominent part in many different dances and games. We all have played Post Office and Spin-the-Bottle in our early years.

Kiss-dances were very common during the Middle Ages and even later. Montaigne describes one that he witnessed at Augsburg in 1580. "The ladies," said he, "sit in two rows along the walls of the room. The gentlemen go over and bow to them; they kiss the ladies' hands, and the ladies get up. Then each gentleman puts his arm round the lady's waist, lays his cheek to hers and kisses her."

One can still take the same liberty at Christmastide under the mistletoe.

But, in the end, a kiss is best employed as an expression and symbol of romantic love.

The Germans have a saying: *Kuss kann man zwar abwischen, aber das Feuer im Herzen nich löschen* (A kiss may indeed be washed away, but the fire in the heart cannot be quenched).

Even so, kisses are not always welcomed, as the nursery rhyme tells us:

Georgie Porgie, pudding and pie,
Kissed the girls and made them cry.

There is a French anecdote of the present day about a student who took the liberty of kissing a young girl. She got very angry, however, and scolded him, whereupon he retorted with irrefutable logic: *Pour Dieu! Mademoiselle ne vous fachez pas. Si ce baiser vous gene, rendez-le-moi* (For goodness' sake, don't be cross, young lady. If that kiss annoys you, give it back to me).

A more amicable settlement was arrived at by a Danish couple who had resolved to break off their engagement: "It is best, I suppose, that we return each other's letters?" said he. "I think so too," replied she, "but shall we not at the same time give each other all our kisses back?" They did so, and thus agreed to renew their engagement.

That one does not arrive at anything by *one* kiss is expressed with sufficient plainness in a Rumanian proverb: *Cu un trat busni nu se afla muliere* (With a single kiss no woman is caught).

And the practiced French add another rule:

Le baiser est un fruit qu'il faut cueiller sur l'arbre (The kiss is a fruit which one ought to pluck from the tree itself).

Annie Laurie

Lady Scott

Love Songs

Andante

p

Max - wel - ton's braes are bon - nie, Where ear - ly fa's the

dew, And 'twas there that An - nie Laur - ie gave me her prom - ise

true; Gave me her prom - ise true; Which ne'er for - got will

be, And for bon-nie An - nie Laur - ie, I'd lay me down and dee.

Her brow is like the-drift, That e'er the sun shone on;
 Her throat is like the swan, And dark blue is her e'e;
Her face it is the fairest And for bonnie Annie Laurie
 That e'er the sun shone on,— I'd lay me down and dee.

My Luve is Like a Red, Red Rose

Robert Burns

O, my luve is like a red, red rose, that's new - ly sprung in June; O, my

luve is like a mel - o - die that's sweet - ly played in tune!

As fair art thou, my bon - nie lass, so deep in luve am I: And

I will luve thee still, my dear, till a' the seas gang dry.

Till a' the seas gang dry, my dear,
    And the rocks melt wi' the sun;
I will luve thee still, my dear,
    While the sands o' life shall run.

And fare thee weel, my only Luve,
    And fare thee weel a while!
And I will come again, my Luve,
    Tho' it were ten thousand mile.

The Passionate Shepherd to His Love

Come live with me and be my love, And we will all the pleas-ures prove, That hills and val-leys, dale and field, And all the crag-gy moun-tains yield. And all the crag-gy moun-tains yield.

And we will sit upon the rocks
    Seeing the shepherds feed their flocks.
By shallow rivers, to whose falls
    Melodious birds sing madrigals.

And I will make thee beds of roses
    And a thousand fragrant posies,
A cap of flowers, and a kirtle
    Embroidered all with leaves of myrtle.

A gown made of the finest wool,
    Which from our pretty lambs we pull,
Fair lined slippers from the cold,
    With buckles of the purest gold.

A belt of straw and ivy buds,
    With coral clasps and amber studs,
And if these pleasures may thee move,
    Come live with me and be my love.

The shepherd swains shall dance and sing
    For thy delight each May morning;
If these delights thy mind may move,
    Come live with me and be my love.

The Seeds of Love

I sowed the seeds of love, It was all in the spring, In A-pril, May, and sun-ny June, When small birds they do sing, When small birds they do sing.

My garden was planted full
 Of flowers everywhere,
But for myself I could not choose
 The flower I held so dear.

In June came the rose so red,
 And that's the flower for me:
But when I gathered the rose so dear,
 I gained but the willow-tree.

I told him I'd take no care
 Till I did feel the smart,
And still did press the rose so dear,
 Till the thorn did piece my heart.

My garden was standing by,
 And he would choose for me:
He chose the primrose, the lily, the pink—
 But those I refused all three.

Oh, the willow-tree will twist,
 And the willow-tree will twine:
And I would I were in the young man's arms
 That ever had this heart of mine.

A posy of hyssop I'll make,
 No other flower I'll touch,
That all the world may plainly see,
 I love one flower too much.

The primrose I did reject
 Because it came too soon;
The lily and pink I overlooked,
 And vowed I would wait till June.

My gardener, as he stood by,
 He bade me take great care,
For if I gathered the rose so red,
 There groweth up a sharp thorn there.

My garden is now run wild;
 When I shall plant anew,
My bed, that once was filled with thyme,
 Is now o'errun with rue.

O Mistress Mine

Believe Me, If All Those Endearing
Young Charms

Thomas Moore

Be - lieve me if all those en - dear - ing young charms, Which I gaze on so fond - ly to - day, Were to

change by to - mor - row and flee from my arms; Like fair - y gifts fad - ing a - way, Thou wouldst

still be a - dored, as this mo-ment thou art, Let thy lov - li - ness fade as it will, And a -

round the dear ru - in, each wish of my heart, Would en - twine it - self ver - dant - ly still.

70

It is not while beauty and youth are thine own,
  And thy cheeks unprofaned by a tear,
That the fervor and faith of a soul may be known,
  To which time will but make thee more dear!

No, the heart that has truly loved never forgets,
  But as truly loves on to the close,
As the sunflower turns to her god when he sets
  The same look which she turned when he rose!

Early One Morning

Traditional English

Softly, and not too slow.

Ear-ly one morn-ing, just as the sun was ris-ing, I heard a maid sing in the val-ley be-low: "Oh, don't de-ceive me! oh, do not leave me! How could you use a poor maid-en so?

"Oh, gay is the garland, and fresh are the roses
  I've culled from the garden to bind on thy brow:
Oh, don't deceive me! oh, do not leave me!
  How could you use a poor maiden so?

"Remember the vows that you made to your Mary;
  Remember the bower where you vowed to be true:
Oh, don't deceive me! oh, never leave me!
  How could you use a poor maiden so?"

Thus sung the poor maiden, her sorrow bewailing,
  Thus sung the poor maid in the valley below:
"Oh, don't deceive me! oh, do not leave me!
  How could you use a poor maiden so?"

Oh! Willow, Willow

—William Shakespeare

Very sad

A poor soul sat sigh-ing by a sy-ca-more tree, Sing wil-low, wil-low, wil-low, With his

hand in his bo-som, and his head up-on his knee, Oh! wil-low, wil-low, wil-low, wil-low, Oh!

wil-low, wil-low, wil-low, wil-low, my gar-land shall be, Sing all a green wil-low,

wil-low, wil-low, wil-low, Ah me, the green wil-low my gar-land shall be.

He sighed in his singing and made a great moan,
  Sing willow, willow, willow,
"I am dead to all pleasure, my true love she is gone,"
  Oh! willow, willow, willow, willow,
Oh! willow, willow, willow, willow, my garland shall be,
  Sing all a green willow, willow, willow, willow,
Ah me, the green willow my garland shall be.

The mute bird sat by him, made tame by his moans,
  Sing willow, willow, willow,
The true tears fell from him and melted the stones,
  Oh! willow, willow, willow, willow,
Oh! willow, willow, willow, willow, my garland shall be,
  Sing all a green willow, willow, willow, willow,
Ah me, the green willow my garland shall be.

Come, all you forsaken, and mourn you with me,
  Sing willow, willow, willow,
Who speaks of a false love, mine's falser than she.
  Oh! willow, willow, willow, willow,
Oh! willow, willow, willow, willow, my garland shall be,
  Sing all a green willow, willow, willow,
Ah me, the green willow my garland shall be.

It Was a Lover and His Lass

William Shakespeare

It was a lov-er and his lass, With a hey, with a ho, with a hey, non-ny

no, and a hey, non-ny no-ni-no; That o'er the green corn-fields did pass In

spring-time, in spring-time, in spring-time, The on-ly pret-ty ring time, When birds do sing, hey

ding a ding a ding, Hey ding a ding a ding, Hey ding a ding a ding, Sweet

lov-ers love the spring!

Between the acres of the rye,
    With a hey, *etc.*
These pretty country folks would lie
    In springtime, *etc.*

This carol they began that hour,
    With a hey, *etc.*
How that life was but a flower
    In springtime, *etc.*

Then, pretty lovers, take the time,
    With a hey, *etc.*
For love is crowned with the prime
    In springtime, *etc.*

Greensleeves

Traditional English

I bought thee kerchers to thy head,
  That were wrought fine and gallantly;
I kept thee both at board and bed,
  Which cost my purse well favoredly.
For oh, Greensleeves, *etc.*

I bought thee petticoats of the best,
  The cloth so fine as might be;
I gave thee jewels for thy chest:
  And all this cost I spent on thee.
For oh, Greensleeves, *etc.*

Thy smock of silk, both fair and white,
  With gold embroidered gorgeously;
Thy petticoat of sendal right:
  And these I bought thee gladly.
For oh, Greensleeves, *etc.*

Greensleeves, now farewell! adieu!
  God I pray to prosper thee!
For I am still thy lover true:
  Come once again and love me!
For oh, Greensleeves, *etc.*

How Should I Your True Love Know?

William Shakespeare

How should I your true love know, From an-o-ther one?

By his cock-le hat and staff, And his san-dal shoon.

He is dead and gone, lady,
　He is dead and gone:
At his head a grass-green turf,
　At his heels a stone.

White his shroud as the mountain snow,
　Larded with sweet flowers,
Which bewept to the grave did go
　With true-love showers.

Drink to Me Only With Thine Eyes

—Ben Jonson

Drink to me on - ly with thine eyes, And I will pledge with mine,

Or leave a kiss with - in the cup, And I'll not ask for wine; The

thirst that from the soul doth rise, Doth ask a drink di - vine;

But might I of Jove's nec - tar sip, I would not change for thine.

I sent thee late a rosy wreath,
  Not so much honouring thee
As giving it a hope that there
  It could not withered be;

But thou thereon didst only breathe
  And send'st it back to me—
Since when it grows and smells, I swear,
  Not of itself, but thee.

Loving
Gifts and
Celebrations
of Tasha
Tudor
and Her
Family

Love is not confined to Valentine's Day in our family or among our friends. There are many occasions all through the year to tell people that you love and appreciate them. Engagements and weddings and their anniversaries are obvious opportunities, as are birthdays. Actually, the nicest thing of all is the unexpected or spontaneous expression of your affection by a word, a home-made gift, a nosegay or token. But still, it is pleasant to have a day set apart specifically for

celebrating love, and the Tudor family has developed many special traditions associated with Valentine's Day.

Valentine's Day in our home centers on the Sparrow Post, where there is always interesting mail on February fourteenth for each member of the family. The Postmaster is Augustus Sparrow. He has served through three generations and is still none the worse for wear. Mr. Sparrow is a cut-wool toy sparrow, made by hand, like many of our favorite characters. He sports a red vest and spectacles. He is very efficient and has coped successfully with many problems during his lifetime, such as lost mail, delayed deliveries, strikes, migration tangles and other trying situations.

The Post Office is refurbished each year. It started out as a grocery carton, but has been turned into quite an elaborate establishment, with cubbyholes for letters, a counter, a set of scales and many important notices pasted to the walls. There is a back office for Mr. Sparrow where he can work in peace and sort the quantities of mail that February fourteenth never fails to bring. The miniature mail is, of course, just the right size for his customers, who are mainly dolls, plush bears, cut-wool rabbits and plush ducklings. There are now several branch offices, including a busy one in Indiana, there being a

considerable rabbit warren there as well as many active and public-minded plush bears.

Valentine production starts as soon as Christmas is over. It takes many hours to make the numbers of small valentines required for this special day. And, of course, each person and each toy character has to receive enough cards to feel warmly loved. Beside the exchanging of the tiny greetings, when the children were little, a whole celebration would be planned for the toys, who were as real to the children, and indeed, to all of us, as if they were truly alive.

Some years, for the ladies' interest, we would have a Fashion Show, featuring the latest styles for dolls, bears, rabbits and ducklings. The favorite of the male members of the family was a Cake Sale, with pretty cardboard booths (see page 85 for directions for making booths) set out with innumerable small cakes, pies, breads and cookies, all most delicious. This is quite easy to do, though somewhat time-consuming. But how greatly it is enjoyed by young visitors!

Some things can be made well ahead of time and frozen until needed. To make the tiny cakes, use your favorite recipe, but bake in cupcake tins or doll kitchen sets. Use small, shallow tart tins for miniature lemon meringue pies. Tiny doughnuts are great favorites. For a festive decoration, string twelve of them on a ribbon to hang from the pillars or roof of your booth. (We use the large end of a cake decorator to cut doughnuts and a small thimble to cut the holes.) We also make doll-sized loaves of bread, and "thimble biscuits"—baking-powder biscuits actually cut with a large, old-fashioned thimble and then baked as usual. Some years we would be very ambitious and make many little bakery boxes in which to place the baked goods. These can be made of thin bristol board or cardboard, cut to a scaled-down pattern of any bakery box that looks simple to cut out and fold together. Small, *really* small, paper bags can often be found in shops,

and it is great fun to look for such items all during the year and store them up, or to make them for Valentine's Day pleasure.

Along with the Cake Booths we always had a Florist's Booth. Making the tiny bouquets is most enjoyable. Use miniature paper lace doilies for the Biedermeiers. There is no end of enchanting

things to do once you set your mind upon it, and if you start early you will have many mornings and afternoons of pleasure with your children and their friends making and filling the booths. Making a Stationery Booth full of tiny valentines and cards is another happy idea.

You will have to use your own imagination to

some extent when making any of these items and you will be surprised how easy they are to make.

A Flower Show was another very popular theme. We used the cake-sale booths, fortunately saved from previous years, for flower displays. These were judged, and desirable prizes awarded the winners. Lovely things can be raised in small pots, such as miniature roses, tiny bulbs, heliotrope and other flowering plants. My children and their friends were enthusiastic pot gardeners.

This kind of project, of course, has to be planned in advance to be sure of blooms at the right time. It is fun to examine the brightly illustrated catalogs during the autumn and winter months, and to order and receive seeds and bulbs to be planted for February flowering. Bulbs must be planted in the fall. If you have a cool cellar, or better still, a cold frame, you can work wonders. Any good gardening book gives thorough information on growing bulbs. The Flower Show is a project that is fun for the entire family, and can lead to a lifetime's interest.

If you wish to be *truly* ambitious and do a memorable long-term project, I'd suggest you give a marionette show. Making the characters, figuring out a simple stage, rehearsing and all the other aspects of producing a marionette show afford endless happy hours. My children, though grown up now, recall with pleasure the fun of past shows. We still do them for the grandchildren.

How to Make Cake-Sale Booths

Obtain a good-sized carton (probably your local grocery store will give you one), tall enough to be in correct proportion to your dolls or bears.

(1) Cut out rectangular openings on three sides only. Cut only the top and two sides of these openings, then score and neatly fold back these flaps or panels to make the floor of the booth. (2) Cut the end lid-flaps in neat triangles, leaving a border of an inch or so along the edges. This can be scored and folded over to support the two sloping, or pitched, sides of the roof, formed from the other two long flaps of the carton top. (3) Find an extra piece of flat cardboard large enough to cover both pitches of the roof. (4)

Score it down the middle so it will bend neatly at the roof's peak. (5) Score again to bend down over the eaves, and cut the edges in a scalloped pattern. (6) Cut two other pieces of flat cardboard to fit across the narrow ends, and scallop the lower edge of each to match the sides. Glue in place.

All parts can be glued or taped together and strengthened with paper wrapping tape. (Do not use plastic tape as this cannot be painted.) Paint the booth white with poster paint. Decorate with pink. If you wish, you can add tiny clear Christmas tree lights for illumination and decoration. This looks especially pretty after dark.

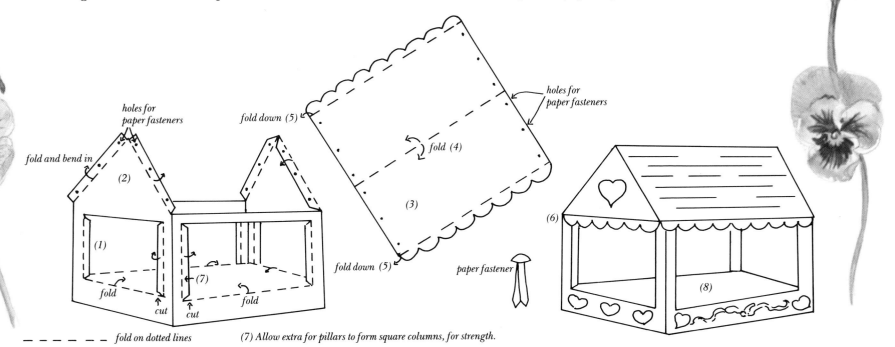

holes for paper fasteners

fold and bend in

(2)

(1)

(7)

fold

cut   cut   fold

- - - - - - - fold on dotted lines

fold down (5)

fold (4)

holes for paper fasteners

(3)

fold down (5)

paper fastener

(6)

(8)

(7) Allow extra for pillars to form square columns, for strength.

(8) Make floor from another piece of cardboard, carefully fitted.

How to Make a Flowerpot Valentine Card

Here is a page to trace in order to make the heart-shaped valentine with pots of flowers. All you need is some good-quality white or pale pink writing paper or drawing paper, some watercolors (Winsor & Newton watercolors are very good), a sable watercolor brush, some paper cement (such as Elmer's glue) and fine-pointed paper-cutting scissors.

Trace and cut out two large hearts, the first one with empty flowerpots, as shown. You may want to scallop the edge of this, or draw lace around the border with a pencil.

Please turn to page 88.

THE LANGUAGE OF FLOWERS. OPEN THIS HEART AND YOU WILL SEE THE FEELINGS THAT I HAVE FOR THEE.

I'm a thief YOU R heart is what I am after!

When dearest I but think of Thee Methinks all things that lovely be are present.

The second large heart is the same size. It is a plain one, to be used for backing. Color the flowerpots (I use Vermilion, a bit of Alizarin Crimson and Burnt Sienna), making them darker on the shadowed side. While your paint is still wet put a touch of bright green here and there to simulate the moss that always grows on clay pots. I make the green by mixing Winsor Blue and Winsor Yellow. Touches of grass are put in with the same green, with strokes of Burnt Sienna and Winsor Blue for accents. (See opposite page.)

Trace the flowers and small hearts on another piece of paper and color them. For the pink azalea, I use Winsor & Newton Rose Doré, with accents of Alizarin Crimson. Various greens can be used for the stems and leaves; I combine Winsor Blue with Winsor Yellow, as above, and add touches of Burnt Sienna. There is a surprising amount of brown in plants. Winsor Violet for the purple hyacinth must be used very carefully. It is a strong color. Winsor Yellow is good for the daffodil's perianth, and Cadmium Yellow for the trumpet. Do try to get a sable brush with a good point, size 5 or 6. And *never* leave your brush standing in water. You will ruin the point if you do.

Have a dish with a paper tissue in it on which to wipe the excess water off your brush.

After painting the flowers, tint the small hearts light red and cut them out, leaving the flowers attached to the hearts. Then cut out the two large hearts, and with a razor blade or crafts knife make slits as marked, along the tops of all the empty pots. Plants and hearts will be inserted in these slits.

With Elmer's glue or rubber cement make a fine line around the outer edge of the large blank heart. Place the large heart with the empty pots on top. Press these between heavy books until glue is dry. While the glue is drying, write bits of poems or loving messages on the small hearts. Now insert the small hearts carefully into the slitted pots on the large heart, leaving the flowers to show as if growing there. Place the taller plants first, putting them to the back.

Imagine the surprise and delight of the recipient when each plant is pulled from its pot to reveal the hidden love notes!

Special Recipes

Frosting

1½ cups granulated
    sugar
½ cup water
2 egg whites, very stiffly
    beaten

1 teaspoon almond
    extract
½ cup maraschino
    cherries, finely
    minced, and a bit of
    their juice

Combine sugar and water. Place on high heat and stir until sugar dissolves. Boil rapidly without stirring until mixture spins a fine thread when dropped from a silver spoon into cold water (238° on a candy thermometer).

Pour sugar syrup in a thin stream over egg whites, while beating constantly. Now add the almond extract and minced maraschino cherries with a bit of their juice. Frost each layer, being mindful to save ample frosting for sides and top of cake when it is assembled. Decorate with young ivy leaves and heart-shaped petals from red or pink geraniums.

Cake recipe is on page 90.

Festive Punch

tea (any good black tea, *not* green)
1¾ cups sugar
1 cup water
juice of 2 oranges (strained) *plus* 3 cups of orange
    juice (strained)
juice of 2 lemons (strained) *plus* 1 cup of lemon juice
    (strained)
juice of 2 limes (strained)
4 sprigs spearmint
1 cup pineapple juice
1 cup of raspberry syrup
    (Try to get Zarex Raspberry Syrup.
    Nothing else tastes as good).
1 quart ginger ale
1 small jar of Maraschino cherries (optional)

Make a quart of plain tea in your usual manner. Mix the juice of 2 oranges, 2 lemons and 2 limes with 1½ cups of the sugar. Add the hot tea to this mixture. Then add 4 sprigs of *real* spearmint. (Do not use orange mint, peppermint or apple mint!) Set mixture aside.

Now mix together the 3 cups of strained orange juice, 1 cup of lemon juice, the pineapple juice, and the raspberry syrup, and combine this with the tea mixture.

Next, boil the remaining ¼ cup of sugar with 1 cup of water for 5 minutes. Add this to the fruit juice and tea mixture. Chill thoroughly. Just before serving, add 1 quart of ginger ale. Serve over a block of ice in a punch bowl. Add sprigs of mint for flavor and decoration. If you wish, you may add a small jar of Maraschino cherries, juice and all.

This makes enough for 30 people. You can keep adding ginger ale if you are running short.

The Tudor Family's Valentine Cake Recipe

8 tablespoons butter
1½ cups granulated sugar
2 eggs, separated

3 cups cake flour
1 cup milk, room temperature
4 teaspoons baking powder
¼ teaspoon salt
1 cup milk, room temperature
1 teaspoon almond extract

You will need two 8-inch round cake pans or two heart-shaped pans about 8-inch size, and also pans for twelve cupcakes. Butter all pans. Preheat oven to 350°. Cream butter thoroughly, add sugar gradually, stirring well after each addition. Next add beaten egg yolks. Stir vigorously. Sift together three times flour, baking powder and salt. Now add dry ingredients alternately with milk, stirring *well* after each addition. Last, add stiffly beaten egg whites. Fold these in with the almond extract for flavoring. Pour the batter into the two larger pans, and into the cupcake pans as well. Bake about 25 minutes, or until cake draws away from the edges of the pans. Turn out on cake rack. When cool, split each large cake, thus making four layers. ♡ ♡ ♡ ♡

Frosting recipe is on
page 89.

How to Make Valentine Bouquets
or
Tussie Mussies

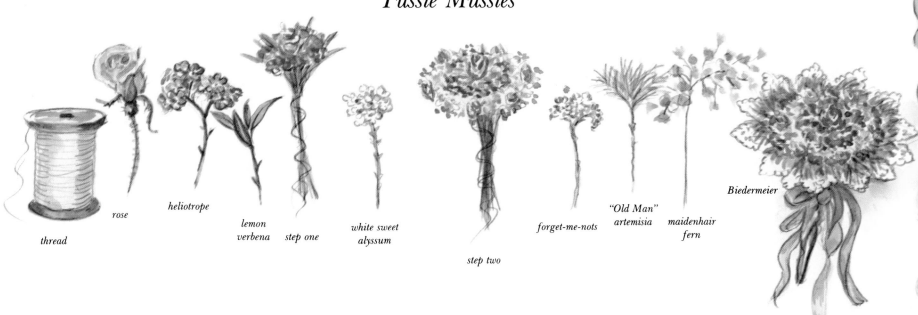

thread

rose

heliotrope

lemon verbena

step one

white sweet alyssum

step two

forget-me-nots

"Old Man" artemisia

maidenhair fern

Biedermeier

step three

To make a Tussie Mussie, gather the needed flowers and herbs (see below) and soak them in a bowl of water for an hour at least. Then strip stems of all leaves and thorns. You will need:

    a spool of thread
    one small rose
    6 sprigs of heliotrope
    4 sprigs of lemon verbena
    8 to 12 sprigs of white sweet alyssum
    12 to 14 sprigs of "Old Man" artemisia
    12 to 14 sprigs of forget-me-nots
    10 to 12 sprigs of maidenhair fern
    4 to 6 tiny rosebuds
    a Biedermeier, or a lace paper doily
    some pretty ribbons

Place the heliotrope and the lemon verbena evenly around the rose and wrap their stems several times with thread (*step one*). Now add a tiny bit of the white sweet alyssum. Next place the rosebuds around these in order, and fill in with forget-me-nots and ferns around the edge as shown (*step two*). Now wrap with more thread until it feels secure.

When thoroughly wrapped, trim off the bottom ends of the stems to match evenly, being careful not to cut your thread. Next put on a Biedermeier. If you can't find Biedermeiers you can use lace paper doilies, cutting a hole in the center for the stems (*step three*). Do, please, avoid plastic ones! They are quite out of keeping. Place your Tussie Mussie in a glass of water and leave in the refrigerator until ready to use. Then remove from water and wrap the stems in a small square of aluminum foil and tie a bow around this using two delicately colored ribbons. Leave long streamers at the ends. You can attach a little card with a special message for the recipient.

Index